Contents

INTRODUCTION

IT MAY SEEM as if there are nearly as many books about sales on the market as there are salespeople. They all promise to make you better at what you do. They all offer variations on similar themes. Many of them have some useful points to make.

But I believe that a key component—an essential factor—in achieving sales mastery has been generally overlooked by self-appointed sales gurus. Through my own hard-won experience and study of the marketplace, I have come to believe that sales mastery depends first and foremost on achieving peerless self-awareness—what I call *Sales Awareness*.

"Know Thyself" was carved into the stone at the entrance of the Temple of Apollo at Delphi, in ancient Greece. This dictum became the foundation of ego transcendence and human self-development through the ages. Clearly, even the ancients understood that discovering one's *true self* was the key to success in every area of life. Applying this to the field of sales, I believe that understanding your true self and unleashing its power can guarantee sales success no matter what you are selling.

Achieving SALES AWARENESS can be as simple as 1-2-3:

1. **Ask great questions.** Great questions position you as a leader and quickly set up an advantageous power dynamic with the customer. They also begin the flow of valuable information in the right direction—from buyer to seller.

2. **Identify and then solve your customer's problems.** Revealing a prospect's pain and then offering valuable

assistance or information to alleviate it compels the buyer to lower his defenses and encourages the prospect's natural tendency to buy, thus fulfilling a need.

3. **Make the sale.** Operating from a position of SALES AWARENESS—awareness of both yourself and your customer—you can close more sales and perform beyond your expectations (and your boss's). It's all about waking up and using that new level of awareness to achieve both your own goals and your customer's. When you're engaged in SALES AWARENESS, sales can be the most satisfying job there is. Are you ready to begin?

Selling

Selling is the greatest occupation on the planet. It combines so many wonderful elements of a happy life: autonomy, creativity, profound human interaction, complexity, challenge, and the potential for unlimited rewards.

My dad was an old-school salesman. After a stint in the Marine Corps, he got a gig selling encyclopedias door to door. Talk about hardcore. He used to tell me stories of people calling the cops on him and having him arrested for soliciting.

Undeterred, he kept at it until he found other sales opportunities that were more lucrative and less stressful. He loved sales. It made sense to him. My dad did not finish college, but that never held him back. He worked hard, but, more important, he worked smart. He was always around for family functions, ball games, and events. And he always had plenty of money for vacations, a nice house, and nice cars. He never seemed to struggle for much of anything.

After some false starts in my early years, working my way through the transportation industry, my dad said to me, "It never made sense to me that a person would go to work and know exactly what they were going to do that day. I prefer a more adventurous approach to life; one where I am in control of my own destiny."

Prior to that, I had never considered following in my father's footsteps, but that statement shook me to my core. I suddenly thought, *What if I were to look into sales as a way to achieve the success I've always wanted? It worked out so well for my father. Why couldn't it work for me?*

I think everyone has a moment or two when, based on a comment, event, speech, or experience, his entire life changes. Well, that was my moment. I had been running around working hard, but I had not been working smart.

I decided right then that I was going to learn how to sell. It was the best decision I ever made. Fortunately, I had the world's greatest salesperson—my dad—as a mentor, but it still took a lot of studying and practice to master it all.

Perhaps like you, I was not born with my dad's gifts. He is a people person and has an uncanny ability to let things go. He never takes offense at anything. In fact, I would say my dad doesn't really understand what rejection is. It is a not factor for him.

I am not that way. I am an introvert. I worry. I have a difficult time letting things go. Rejection hurts me deeply. These are not the classic qualities of a great salesperson. Yet, with time, patience, study, self-awareness, and practice, I have been able to work through these issues. The point is, if I could overcome my insecurities and become a successful salesperson, so can you.

The Greatest Profession

In my opinion, knowing how to sell is the single most important skill to have in any field, without exception. Selling is nothing more than seeing the value in something and then being able to communicate that value to another person in a way that moves him to act. No matter what you do, you could undoubtedly use that skill.

There is a myth out there that owning your own business is the only way to find satisfaction and take control of your life and finances. I totally disagree. Sales is the other option, and it is a better one. Much better. Much, much, much better.

Besides being an entrepreneur, sales is the only occupation I can think of that allows you to enjoy an unlimited potential for income—and even business owners face the inescapable reality that much of their time is spent selling. Ask any one of them. And then ask him about the burden of overseeing production and distribution, dealing with shrinkage or theft, handling bookkeeping, accounting, personnel issues, fraud, healthcare, lawsuits, returns, overhead, and the rest. Still think owning a business is the golden ticket?

In sales, all you have to worry about is selling. Once you've undergone some good training and summoned up some self-discipline, sales can provide you with unlimited income as well as the time and energy to spend on family, friends, hobbies, adventures, travel, or anything else your heart desires. I truly believe it's the path to genuine work/life balance.

Training and Self-Discipline

I have heard plenty of horror stories from people who have attempted a career in sales. I get it. I had to go through some terrible times myself. It can be rough in the beginning. But so is anything worthwhile. Nobody said it would be a walk in the park.

Remember learning how to ride a bike? I bet you suffered a few scraped knees and perhaps a bruised ego, but you pushed through and mastered the skill. The challenges in sales can be overcome in the same way.

Rejection can be painful, and there is a lot of it in sales, but when you weigh the pluses and minuses, sales is a winner. After a little training and practice, sales can be an incredibly lucrative and rewarding occupation. And when the successes start rolling in, the thrill of closing a sale is hard to beat. Talk to any experienced salesperson and he will tell you how exhilarating closing a big sale can be.

And the opportunities! See for yourself. Go to any employment service, jobs website, or classified page and look at the sales section. Opportunities abound. Corporations all over the world are screaming for skilled salespeople.

Sales principles apply whether you are selling business-to-business consumer goods, online, offline, over the phone, door-to-door, or to big audiences. You have to grab and hold the buyer's attention. You have to inspire interest. You have to develop desire. And you have to move the prospect to BUY.

Genuine Security

If you can sell, you will always have a job and be successful. And then there are the opportunities beyond sales! Once you have established your sales skills, doors will open to you all over town. More CEOs and COOs come from the sales department than any other.

The key is the ability to communicate the essential value of any situation, product, or service and move people to act. If you can do that, you become extremely valuable to others.

Sales is the premium path to success, and this book will guide you step by step. To get started, you just need a few secrets and a little training.

I committed myself to learning the art and science of selling, and you should, too. Once I learned the basics and started closing sales, I never looked back—and selling got easier and easier. It is entirely possible for the same thing to happen to you. Since I started selling, I have never had to struggle for a dollar or worry about money. I wish the same for you, and this book is going to help you get to that point.

I'm guessing that since you are reading this, you are a salesperson by profession or would like to be. But whether or not that is true, you engage in sales in some form all the time—we all do. So you may as well get really, really good at it, don't you think?

That said, selling has never been more difficult than it is right now. Over time, massive physical and psychological walls have emerged to keep sales messages and salespeople at bay. In my considered opinion, the best way to break through these defensive barriers is to keep in mind the important principles of SALES AWARENESS and use them to understand your buyer's perspective. You can then solve his problems, contribute to his sense of well-being—and make more sales.

The starting point of this process is to ask powerful questions. In this way, you can control the sales call and understand the buyer's perspective. This, in turn, positions you as a valuable resource and a leader whom the buyer can trust. You will also be earning his respect and his appreciation of your value proposition. If that value proposition is perceived as truly problem-solving and valuable, the sales cycle can and will conclude with a win-win result.

Unique in the literature of sales techniques, *Sales Awareness* combines cutting-edge technical sales skills with ancient philosophical and developmental wisdom. The result is an astonishingly easy-to-follow strategy for success in both sales and life.

Read on to begin your personal transformation.

CONTEXT: THE HISTORY OF SALES

Pre-Internet Age

SALESPEOPLE HAVE ALWAYS GOTTEN A BAD RAP—and for a long time, it was probably deserved. Before the advent of the Internet, the typical salesperson felt free to behave like a manipulative, slimy, dishonest, pushy creep. Hawkers, door-to-door salesmen, and used car salesmen glad-handed, ABC'd (Always Be Closing), lied, exaggerated, and cheated their way through their sales calls, preying on unsuspecting and ill-informed buyers. Generally speaking, their results—no matter how dramatic—could be characterized as "win-lose" sales.

The Internet changed all that by changing the balance of power. Customers have become better informed than ever. Salespeople no longer have the upper hand when it comes to imparting information about a product or service. It takes but a few keystrokes on a phone, tablet, or computer to instantly verify a salesperson's claim about a product—as well as to check up on the reputation of the company and the satisfaction of its customers.

Buyers now have the power of information at their fingertips and can make their own decisions about what to buy, when to buy it, and whom to buy it from—without help from a sleazy salesperson whose aim is to push them to buy unwanted and unneeded items. The argument could even be made (and it has been) that salespeople are obsolete.

But I don't believe that for a minute.

Internet Age

As the information balance of power shifted from sellers to buyers, a new selling philosophy was born. "Consultative Selling" has given the sales industry new hope that it is still relevant in the new, information-driven world order.

Consultative selling is a strategy whereby the seller works *with* the buyer to glean important details regarding that buyer's needs, wants, objections, negotiations, and perspective. The process is meant to turn an adversarial relationship into a collaborative one, and it is a massive leap in evolution from the manipulative "used-car sales" tactics of the past.

When deployed well, consultative selling yields a win-win sale every time. But when deployed poorly, consultative selling is dishearteningly ineffective and can result in the worst result imaginable to a salesperson: lose-win sales. In these cases, the buyer wins but the seller loses, due to ever-increasing pressure to commoditize any and all products and services. In other words, the sales call has devolved into a negotiation—usually over price or availability—and the seller has placed himself in a no-win situation.

Most of the consultative sales tactics taught today are throwbacks to the great Dale Carnegie and Zig Ziglar, whose consultative sales training strategies were adopted by huge corporations such as Xerox and IBM and soon became so ubiquitous that almost everyone can recognize when they are being "sold." In fact, customers often understand the strategies better than the novice salespeople using them.

Salespeople still using these time-tested but somewhat tired old methods tend to drown in frustration, daunted by low productivity. Intuitively, they know that it is time for something new—a new strategy infused with integrity and simplicity. It is time for a sales strategy that will lead to higher productivity, fewer closed doors, and fewer unreturned phone calls.

Sales Awareness: Professional Sales Essentials

The SALES AWARENESS selling strategy I outline in this book is consultative at its core, but streamlined for more efficient, foolproof implementation that can ensure sales success.

I will say it again, because it can't be stated too often: In today's selling environment, the seller must work *with* the buyer. He must ask great questions and listen to the answers. He must strive for a deep understanding of the buyer's perspective and business.

Then and only then can the seller present solutions to the buyer's problems, products that fill his needs, and value that speaks to his pains and problems rather than simply reflecting the seller's own desires.

Consultative selling was an important theory in its day, and it remains a great foundation for any salesperson to have. But today's sales calls operate on a different playing field, and new moves are called for—solid, practical, effective maneuvers that keep the seller in control and lead to a win-win result.

This brief, user-friendly manual maps out the essential principles, strategies, processes, and procedures of what I call SALES AWARENESS in straightforward language and with illustrative anecdotes. I hope it leads you to great success, whatever your selling environment, and that the skills you attain here will serve you well for a lifetime.

FUNDAMENTALS, PART 1: POWER DYNAMICS AND THE MOST IMPORTANT QUESTIONS

Question 1: *Who is in control of the sales call?*
Answer: *The person asking the questions is in control of the sales call.*

Question 2: *Who thinks he is in control of the sales call?*
Answer: *The person doing the most talking. It relaxes him and encourages him to share valuable information.*

WHAT'S MY POINT? You talk too much. Stop doing that. It is killing your sales efforts.

The first thing you must understand is this: The most important power dynamic in sales is controlling the sales call—and nine times out of ten, you are starting at a disadvantage. Most sales meetings are at the buyer's office, on the buyer's turf, where the buyer is king.

As the seller, you are typically seen as a lowly peddler, hawking unneeded products or services. This dynamic must be overcome in the first few seconds of a sales call or it will dictate all that follows. How can you change it? By asking intriguing and relevant questions.

Keep in mind that the buyer is a decision-maker, accustomed to "being the boss" and dismissing anything that does not address the immediate needs of his business. He is looking for a reason to get rid of you and get back to the work you interrupted.

Your first job is to overcome the image of the "used-car salesman" pushing something on him that he doesn't need or want, and prove your immediate value to him. You do this by drawing him out. Ask great questions. Display leadership qualities of your own. Engage him. Rather than simply *presenting*, be fully *present*—and demand that he be present as well.

The Five Most Important Questions Every Business Leader Needs to Answer for Himself

So what are these all-important questions? Well, think about it. The buyer—your potential client—has problems and is looking for solutions. Whether he knows it or not, he needs a leader to guide him toward those solutions.

When you ask buyer-centric questions, you are presenting yourself as that leader—as someone who understands his problems and can solve them. So, you must start by asking yourself *the same questions he is asking himself* in order to understand his business and help him solve his problems.

Initially, you may not be able to answer those questions with any specificity—but trying to figure out the answers to them prior to any engagement with him will provide you with valuable insight into his needs.

Knowing that your customer is struggling with these important questions puts you miles ahead of your competition. Most salespeople do not consider the bigger-picture needs of the companies they are selling to. This is a fatal error. Think about it: One of the keys to being a successful salesperson is being able to see how your product or service serves a business's mission, addresses its customer base, enhances its product value, and contributes to its success. To see all this, you must delve deeply into the same concerns your customer faces on a daily basis, and emerge with answers.

Mastering the art and science of selling includes communicating to the customer where and how your product fits into his business context. According to the world-renowned management consultant Peter Drucker, these are the five most important questions every business leader needs to answer for himself:

- What is your mission?
- Who is your customer?
- What does your customer value?
- What are your results?
- What is your plan?

Helping your customer answer these questions will position you as a leader. They are great questions with which to begin a sales call, because they are the very questions the buyer is grappling with in his own professional life.

The Five Most Important Questions Every Salesperson Needs to Answer During the Sales Process

It isn't just the business leader's questions (and potential answers) that are important; there is another set of questions that is equally crucial to the process. These are the questions you must ask—and find answers to—during the sales process.

In addition to changing the power dynamic to make it more favorable to you (the seller), posing these questions to your customer will provide you with information critical to making the sale. Always make sure you are laser-focused on discovering:

- What is the buyer's problem
  or issue that needs solving?
- What is the buyer's budget?

- What is the buyer's timeframe?
- What is the buyer's buying process, and why?
- Who is really making the decisions?

If you've determined the answers to these questions, you can be sure you are controlling the meeting and you are probably on the path to a successful sale. If you don't manage to take control of the meeting and the buyer ends up driving it, chances are it will deteriorate into a negotiation on price or availability. Once that happens, you can no longer sell value. You've abdicated your most important and effective function.

Throughout this book, I recommend questions inspired by Gerhard Gschwandtner's fantastic book, *Sales Questions That Close Every Deal: 1000 Field-Tested Questions to Increase Your Profits*. For each phase of the sales call, I have suggested many questions that you can use verbatim—but I would encourage you to create your own as well, and also to look more deeply into Gschwandtner's amazing resource. It is a worthy companion to this book; you would be wise to purchase it and refer to it often.

FUNDAMENTALS, PART 2: THE SALES PITCH OR SALES PRESENTATION

As IMPORTANT AS THOSE ALL-POWERFUL questions can be, they must be accompanied by a good sales pitch or presentation. As you probably know, the sales pitch is the most versatile and significant tool in the salesperson's toolbox, so it pays to put a lot of thought into it.

If crafted well, your sales pitch will do the majority of the work for you, and you'll rarely want to stray from it. But keep in mind as you craft it that *less is more*. You only want to be doing around 20 percent of the talking during any sales call; your buyer should be taking up 80 percent of the airtime.

With that in mind, a foolproof sales pitch is a buyer-focused, one-page, two-to-three-minute speech divided into five short sections. It should present a solution to the buyer's emotional pain, needs, or problems. (The answers to the questions you have already asked will help you refine your pitch on the spot, as needed.) For more on this topic, you can read Mark Weinberg's *New Sales. Simplified*—but I've outlined the basics below.

The five elements that every sales pitch or presentation should contain are:

1. An introductory statement
2. A transition statement
3. A list of problems
4. A description-of-services statement
5. A list of differentiators

Now let's talk about each one of these in a little more detail.

1. Introductory Statement

The introductory statement consists of one to three sentences that inform the buyer who you are and who you represent. Keep this short and simple.

Example: *My name is Max Seller. I represent ACME Widget Company. We produce computer widgets.*

2. Transition Statement

The transition statement captivates the buyer by persuading him right off the bat that you are focused on the issues most important to him. This should be a third-person statement of fact rather than a claim of some kind.

Example: *Companies like yours turn to ACME Widget Company to solve…*

3. List of Problems

This is a list of two to six problems faced by your buyer. You've identified them based on your research and probing (and just plain intuition), and they prove that you understand the buyer's needs, pains, and problems. This list also piques the buyer's interest in you, personally, and positions you as a credible solution agent.

Example:

1. Efficiency Issues
2. Regulatory Pain
3. Time Pressure
4. Mechanical Needs
5. Operational Problems
6. Threat Situations
7. Competition Pressure

8. Process Issues
9. Customer Pain
10. Etc.

4. Description-of-Services Statement

This is another short (one- to two-sentence) statement that describes what you sell. Understand that this is the least interesting element of your sales pitch, and it should be framed as a simple statement of fact rather than used as an opportunity to blather endlessly about how great your company or product is.

Critical point: The buyer does not care what you sell. The buyer only cares about what you can do for him.

Example: *The ACME Widget Company makes widgets. Our widgets come in a variety of colors in sizes small, medium, and large.*

5. List of Differentiators

This is a list of two to six things that set your product or service apart from all others on the market—in a good way, of course. Always remember to include a benefit to the customer for every differentiator.

Example:

1. We have more colors, which means more variety for you and your customers.
2. We have more sizes, which gives you more options.
3. We ship overnight so you can benefit right away.
4. We provide thirty days of unlimited customer support so you can be sure your questions are answered.
5. We have a ninety-day money back guarantee, so you can rest easy about your choice.

6. Our quality-control department is nationally recognized by the BBB, so you can be sure you are buying from a reputable company.
7. No payment for thirty days provides financial flexibility while you learn to utilize your new widget.
8. Etc.

Mini Sales Pitches

Now that you have crafted, memorized, and mastered your sales pitch or presentation, it is important to create a number of mini sales pitches you can use in varying circumstances. Remember, during your initial sales calls, your main strategy should be to elicit information and ask great questions. Inevitably, the information you glean from this process will necessitate adjustments to your pitch.

Since it is your goal to be extremely responsive to your buyer, you must be nimble and adept at adjusting—and even be able to improvise on the spot if necessary. Good and thorough preparation—doing your homework—plus practice and experience are what makes this possible.

That said, this seems a good time to repeat an important point: Your prospect will get bored and lose interest if you talk too much. The good news is, the better prepared you are, the more succinct you can be.

Mini sales pitches can keep you focused and on-message, and prevent you from talking too much while reinforcing the essence of your selling effort. Using your basic sales pitch as a base, develop six or more different mini sales pitches.

You might think of these as advertising slogans. After all, advertisers are salespeople too. They use these short, pithy slogans to gain attention quickly and embed key aspects of their product into the customer's psyche. Here are some examples from Daniel H. Pink's *To Sell Is Human* to get you started. Have them ready for any situation, not just formal sales calls.

The One-Word Sales Pitch
Reduce your sales pitch to the most essential element—just one word—and repeat it often. Here are some real-world examples:
- UPS: *Logistics*
- IBM: *Think*
- Acura: *Advance*
- HP: *Invent*
- Samsung: *Imagine*

The Question Sales Pitch
This one can help you engage the buyer more fully. Just make sure you know what the answer will be, and that it is the answer you want. Here are some real-world examples:
- Capital One: *What's in your wallet?*
- California Milk Processor Board: *Got Milk?*
- Ford: *Have you driven a Ford lately?*
- Verizon: *Can you hear me now?*
- Wendy's: *Where's the beef?*
- Good Humor-Breyers: *What would you do for a Klondike Bar?*

The Rhyming Sales Pitch
Rhyming sales pitches are catchy and stick in buyers' heads. Here are some real-world examples:

- KIX Cereal: Kids like KIX for what KIX has got. Moms like KIX for what KIX has not.
- Alka Seltzer: Plop, plop, fizz, fizz, oh what a relief it is.
- Yahoo: Do you Yahoo?
- Motorola: Hello Moto.
- Pringles: Once you pop, you can't stop.
- Pillsbury: Nothin' says lovin' like somethin' from the oven.
- Pepperidge Farm Goldfish: The snack that smiles back.

The E-mail Subject Line Sales Pitch

For many buyers, e-mail is the preferred method of communication. It is important to know how to use e-mail effectively, and the subject line can be a great opportunity for a pitch, since it probably sits in front of the buyer's eyes all day long.

This pitch should be either intriguing or work-related. *Intriguing* subject lines work best on buyers with a light e-mail load. *Work-related* subject lines work best on buyers with a heavy e-mail load. Here are some examples:

- Do you know about the sales success checklist?
- Top ten strategies to get your e-mail read.
- The 7 biggest mistakes business leaders make when hiring.
- I have your ticket.
- Have you seen this?
- Is your business suffering from lack of cash flow?

The Twitter Sales Pitch

Social media can be a very effective and efficient way to reach the masses with your sales message—and of course Twitter is based on a message length of no more than 140 characters. This is plenty for an effective sales pitch; just whittle down your larger pitch to a few pithy lines that are both problem-solving and buyer-centric. Here are a couple of examples:

> *If you're struggling with your business, then take a quick moment to look over this business-critical information.*

> *FYI. I completed a new report this last week. It details some "insider strategies" that I personally use to boost my sales success.*

The Story Pitch

Everyone loves a good story, and stories are easy to remember, which makes the story format a good way to pitch your product or service in some contexts. Barbara Minto, formerly of the consulting firm McKinsey and Company, uses the following template for her business presentations.

> *Once upon a time_____. Every day_____.*
> *One day_____. Because of that, _____.*
> *Because of that,_____. Until finally_____.*

Here's an example, using this book as the product:

> *Once upon a time, a salesperson struggled to sell. Every day he met with rejection, in person and on the phone. One day, the salesperson discovered SALES AWARENESS and decided to follow its principles. Because of that, he learned how to ask great questions and solve buyers' problems. Because*

of that, he became extremely successful. Until finally, the salesperson doubled his sales over the previous quarter and made a handsome profit.

FUNDAMENTALS, PART 3: SELF-AWARENESS

NOW WE GET TO THE CRUX OF THIS BOOK, the concept that gives it its name. *Awareness.* Self-awareness is essential to your success, so we'll start there.

More than any sales technique or strategy, self-awareness is far and away the most important aspect of your personal and professional development. Even if you were to work solely on self-awareness, you would vastly improve your sales success rate—and here's why.

Your current station in life is a result of your sense of self-worth or self-concept. Long ago, you unconsciously decided exactly how much success you would attain in this lifetime, and you have been on a path toward that point ever since. But perhaps you didn't aim high enough. Perhaps, without even realizing it, you sold yourself short.

Self-worth is like the ocean tide that effortlessly raises all the boats in the harbor. Raise your self-worth and you will automatically expect and receive more out of every facet of your life.

To increase your sense of self-worth, you must develop your self-awareness. Attempting to elevate your self-worth without developing self-awareness is like attempting to fill the harbor at low tide with a garden hose. To put it mildly, this is not the best way to raise the boats! It might have some small effect, but it will never get you very far.

There are thousands of books on self-awareness, by authors who come at the topic from various disciplines: spirituality, psychology, philosophy, religion, even business. One of these approaches is bound to resonate with you. I suggest that you visit the self-help section of your local bookstore and start reading the books that appeal to you, based on your own beliefs and background.

The Cherokee Legend

The Cherokee legend known as "Two Wolves" is a great place to begin your study of self-awareness, so I'll paraphrase it here.

A Cherokee elder is teaching his grandson about life. "A fight is going on inside me," he says to the boy. "It is a terrible fight and it is between two wolves. One is evil. He is anger, envy, sorrow, regret, greed, arrogance, self-pity, guilt, resentment, inferiority, lies, false pride, superiority, and ego.

"The other is good," he continues. He is joy, peace, love, hope, serenity, humility, kindness, benevolence, empathy, generosity, truth, compassion, and faith. The same fight is going on inside you, my child, and inside every person you meet."

The grandson thinks about this for a minute, then asks his grandfather, "Which wolf will win?"

"The one you feed," replies the wise man.

This legend tells us that we are born with two natures, two identities from which we operate daily. And when you think about it, it rings true. Surely, you've noticed that on any given day, you can be forgiving, kind, and generous—while the next day you might be mean, nasty, and greedy. What is going on?

The Ego/True Self

The way I see it, we all have within our psyches two operating systems, much like a PC and a Mac. Both can compute, but they do it in very different ways. What most do not realize is that one of our operating systems is perfect (the True Self), and the other is terribly flawed (the False Self/Ego).

Your True Self is perfect, always doing and saying the right things in the right way, never needing psychological stroking and never taking offense at anything. This self never worries and is always fearless. This self—your True Self—is always available to operate your personality, body, and mind. You just have to get into the habit of using this operating system. You can do this by developing self-awareness.

Your False Self/Ego is holding you back. If you take the time to investigate, you will see that your Ego identity is nothing more than an idea you were taught to buy into. It is only concerned with itself and with protecting what amounts to a basket of preferences. The Ego has gone through life picking up random ideas that it thought were critical for its survival.

You may be a Green Bay Packers fan or prefer heads over tails in a coin toss or like the Beatles and not the Rolling Stones. Whatever your preferences are on a wide array of issues, including your self-worth, your Ego will defend those preferences to the death whenever they are questioned.

If your self-worth preference is extremely low, your Ego will defend that thinking and prevent you from improving yourself. The Ego needs lots of strokes, gets offended easily, tires easily, worries incessantly, and says or does the wrong things at the wrong times over and over because it needs to protect its low self-image.

In a sales situation, if you are identified with your True Self, you will intuit brilliant things to say and observe almost imperceptible notions about the buyer that your Ego could or would never see. The Ego is too wrapped up in its own worries, judgments, and needs to see what is clearly visible to your True Self.

Rejection is another area in which the True Self dominates. While the Ego might be ready to quit sales forever at the first sign of rejection because of its pathetic fragility and its need to protect itself at all costs, the True Self is unconcerned with rejection and can work through it, rise above it, and ultimately prevail.

Since rejection is something a salesperson must learn to deal with on a daily basis, it is essential that he learn to listen to his True Self rather than his Ego as he goes about his work.

The True Self does not take offense at rejection because the True Self does not take things personally. It has no preference. It simply lets things like rejection slide on by as easily as a kid slides down a slip-n-slide.

Your Ego Is Keeping You from Succeeding

Most people are stuck in the same place their whole lives. They basically look the same, weigh the same, have the same amount of money in their bank accounts regardless of how much they make, have the same relationship problems no matter who they are with, and on and on.

The sad fact is that all of them know deep down that they were meant to lead better, more productive lives, but they cannot figure out how to break through and live up to their immense potential.

At certain points in their lives, when they are determined to change, they might lose some weight or sock away a few more dollars; but before long, they gain that weight back or find themselves living paycheck to paycheck again. Every bit of progress seems to slip away no matter how many self-help books they read or how many new diets, savings strategies, or business techniques they try.

What is going on?

The answer is, their Egos are holding them down. If you want to change—truly change for good and for the better—stop identifying with your Ego. Then and only then, *everything* will change for you.

A, B, and C People

For the sake of delving deeper into the function of Ego, let's divide everyone into three basic types: A, B, and C.

A-type people are amazing. They have for the most part left their Egos behind and seem to succeed regardless of their circumstances. Take away their bank accounts, loved ones, jobs, or anything else, and they will always rise back to the top. They are easy to work with, never complain, and look forward to any challenge you can throw at them. These people are living from their True Selves.

A-type people are virtually guaranteed to succeed in sales, or anything else for that matter. When you develop your self-awareness, you become an A-type person.

B-type people get by. They largely live from their Egos but experience random flashes of their True Selves. They do the minimum necessary to continue living as they currently do—no more, no less.

B-type people might occasionally have a great week in sales, but eventually they regress back to their comfortable place on the sales team, usually middle to low in the pack. Should a B-type person discover that he is going to miss his quota, he spends the last day miraculously selling like a champ—because his comfort level is near the middle. He cannot bear to fall below a certain level of performance, any more than he can rise up and become a star.

B-type people sometimes get sent to sales training courses, and they improve for a bit. But before long they return to their old comfort level, no matter how great the training. Unless they learn to break away from their Egos, they are doomed to remain at the same level of success and achievement.

C-type people are worthy of pity but not much else, so I'm not going to spend much time on them. This book is not intended for them, and it's unlikely that any of them are reading it. Most C-type people cannot hold onto a job or relationship and eventually resign themselves to a life on the margins. There are professionals out there devoted to helping these people, but I'd prefer to expend my energy on those with genuine potential to learn, improve, and succeed.

If you are an A-type, you recognize that there is always room for improvement and you are willing to do what it takes to be the best you can be. If you are a B-type, congratulations! Reading this book might help you most of all, since you have recognized that there is more out there for you if you hone your skills.

I hope that at this point you understand the nature of True Self and all of the success that can come from living in accord with it, rather than succumbing to Ego. I applaud your efforts and encourage you to develop the self-awareness necessary to live a life liberated from the Ego's tortured manifestations.

Positive Affirmations

I feel compelled to say a few words about positive affirmations—those positive words and phrases we repeat to ourselves when we need a shot of encouragement that the world seems to be denying us.

They don't work.

They don't do any harm, but really—they don't work.

I am reminded of the old *Saturday Night Live* skits with Al Franken as Stuart Smalley. They always ended with Stuart looking in the mirror and saying, "I'm good enough, I'm smart enough, and gosh darn it, people like me."

The reason that skit is so funny is that deep down, we all know that this method of increasing self-worth is bogus beyond belief. Why? Because positive affirmations attempt to use the Ego to transcend the Ego. The Ego cannot fix itself. It is fundamentally flawed. The whole of the Ego is the problem. Trying to fix it just creates more problems.

It takes something much more powerful, something from a much higher level of consciousness, to propel you out of your current level of understanding and existence.

As Albert Einstein said, "No problem can be solved from the same level of consciousness that created it."

Using positive affirmations to increase your self-worth is like trying to solve a multi-variable calculus equation by using your fingers and toes to count to 20 (if you are blessed to have that many phalanges).

I'm not saying that positive affirmations are harmful. You are certainly better off telling yourself, "I ROCK," rather than, "I SUCK." But if you are intent on changing your life in extremely profound ways, building your self-worth by developing your self-awareness—striving for a state of SALES AWARENESS—will produce much better results than mumbling encouraging words into the mirror.

To get back to the context of sales: Working from the True Self perspective will ultimately make the sales process easier for both you and your customer. I urge you to work on self-awareness.

Practice focusing on the present moment. Read any and all self-help books that strike your fancy. Take to heart the lesson of the Cherokee elder. Become as self-aware as you can. This, above all else, will improve your sales success.

Beyond dedicated and disciplined self-awareness study, here are a couple of simple but extremely powerful techniques that will help you stay aligned with your True Self in any sales situation.

Techniques For Aligning Yourself With Your True Self

How can you operate from your True Self? The answer is so simple it may not seem significant: *Increase your level of awareness, come awake, and be present.* Use your physical senses to come awake to the present moment, where your True Self always resides.

Your Ego cannot survive in the present moment; it can only live in the past and future. It cannot tolerate an increase of awareness, any type of awareness, including something as simple as remembering to use your peripheral vision. Your Ego depends on you being oblivious to your surroundings.

You can increase your awareness right now by doing any or all of these things:

- Pay attention to the sounds around you.
- Pay attention to the smells around you.
- Pay attention to the temperature and the wind on your skin.
- Pay attention to the taste in your mouth.
- Pay attention to your peripheral vision.
- Pay attention to how you are sitting.
- Pay attention to the look on your face.

- Pay attention to the thoughts running through your head.
- Pay attention to your breathing.

These simple methods of coming awake will increase your awareness of your True Self, and in turn, of your prospect's intentions, wishes, needs, worries, fears, and pains. And the best part is, you can practice this discipline any time at all, without anyone knowing you are doing it. It is like having a secret superpower.

I promise you that these techniques, when applied diligently, will increase your sales success exponentially. Use them as frequently as possible during sales calls—or any time. Striving for SALES AWARENESS is a great habit to develop.

List of Self-Development Authors
I could devote a whole book to the topic of self-awareness, but that isn't my purpose—and why should it be, when so many brilliant thinkers have trodden that ground before me? But before we move on to the nuts and bolts of selling, I'd like to offer you my personal "power list" of authors and teachers who have facilitated extraordinary self-awareness breakthroughs for me.

These innovators pass the "my house is burning and I can only take a few books" test. If you are interested in learning more about *self-awareness, self-concept*, and *self-worth*, I encourage you to explore their many published works.

Dale Carnegie
Considered the innovator of consultative sales philosophy, Carnegie set the bar for sales training, public speaking, self-improvement, and

interpersonal skills. His groundbreaking books *How to Win Friends and Influence People* and *Stop Worrying and Start Living* were runaway bestsellers throughout the twentieth century, and they remain popular today. Carnegie doesn't specifically point to the Ego as the root of one's problems, but his methods for discovering and influencing human behavior require an essentially Ego-less approach. I have yet to read a self-help book that does not rely heavily on Carnegie's original work (or that of Napoleon Hill, below). It is instructive as well as inspiring to see where the great ideas originated.

Napoleon Hill

Hill is best known for his book *Think and Grow Rich*. For this classic, he interviewed the most significant early-twentieth-century captains of industry, including Thomas Edison, Henry Ford, and Andrew Carnegie (no relation to Dale). Influenced most by Carnegie, Hill discovered the underlying behaviors and motivations of these great human beings and passed it along in *Think and Grow Rich*. Wouldn't you like to know how the most influential people of the last century attained their success? You can find out in this groundbreaking book. *www.naphill.org*

Earl Nightingale

Nightingale built upon the works of Napoleon Hill and Andrew Carnegie to become a huge influence on today's self-help movement. A voracious collector of great ideas, his ability to recognize truly talented people capable of transforming lives for the better was uncanny. Check out almost anything from the wonderful Nightingale-Conant collection. *www.nightingale.com*

Henry David Thoreau
A prolific writer in the mid-1800s, Thoreau is best known for his book, *Walden*. He had a gift for challenging conventional wisdom on just about any topic, and his timeless pearls of wisdom are as relevant today as they were almost two centuries ago. If you have ever felt the need to simplify your life, read a little Thoreau and you will suddenly find the motivation to de-couple yourself from the complicated, Ego-centered life.
https://www.walden.org/

Ralph Waldo Emerson
Emerson is by far my favorite classic literary figure. Considered the father of Transcendentalism, he is another classic author from the 1800s whose message remains perpetually current. Transcendentalism was a movement dedicated to "transcending" the Ego. Emerson's treatise on Self-Reliance presents an eloquent counterpoint to the modern world's addiction to victimhood and the victim mentality. Much of his work could be considered progressive today, though it was written a century and a half ago.

Wayne Dyer
Dr. Wayne Dyer is probably the most modern and mainstream author on my list. He is a well-known motivational speaker and teacher who has written insightful books such as *The Power of Intention* and *Excuses Begone!* Dyer's gift is his ability to expose the Ego for the destructive fraud that it is. Dyer comes across like a gentle, wise old counselor who knows every move you are going to make before you make it. He is a great resource for real life, down-to-Earth wisdom.
http://www.drwaynedyer.com/

Vernon Howard
In my opinion, Vernon Howard (1918–1992) is easily the clearest communicator of self-awareness ideas on the planet. If I could choose only one author to read in order to gain the deepest understanding of the human condition and how to improve it, it would be Howard. Others are more verbose, but none are more accessible.
http://www.anewlife.org/html/vernon_howard.html

Guy Finley
Largely influenced by Vernon Howard, Guy Finley has taken up the torch and continues to run with it. He does a fantastic job of identifying the characteristics of the Ego and prescribing effective strategies for limiting its influence.
http://www.guyfinley.org/

Dr. David R. Hawkins
If you are interested in graduate or even post-graduate level studies in psychology and self-awareness, Dr. Hawkins is your guy. He developed a kinesiological test for calibrating the integrity of "everything." Most people who read Hawkins get caught up in calibrating things, which is virtually impossible to do accurately unless you are fully enlightened. My advice, at least initially, is to simply trust his calibrations and simply immerse yourself in some of the most advanced spiritual study ever written. His later books are much more focused on practical steps for recognizing and limiting the Ego's influence on your life.
http://veritaspub.com/

Ken Wilber

Probably the greatest philosopher of our time—literally a genius—
Ken Wilber would impress even the likes of Plato, Plotinus, Socrates,
and Aristotle. His greatest contribution to self-awareness studies is
the context he provides. In his brilliant "AQAL Integrated Map,"
Wilber encapsulates human consciousness and all its manifestations. He is the master of weaving and synthesizing all religions,
philosophies, and psychologies. If you want a Masters degree in
theology, save your money and time and read a few of Ken Wilber's
books or listen to a few of his talks.
AQAL Map:
http://revolutionmagik.files.wordpress.com/2010/06/
aqal_map_screen4.jpg
Ken Wilber's website:
http://www.kenwilber.com/home/landing/index.html

Thomas Merton

Thomas Merton (1915–1968) was a Catholic Trappist Monk and an
incredibly courageous writer for his time. Immersed in the Catholic
world of pre-modern thinking, doctrine, and dogma, Merton wrote
some of the most visionary and enlightened religious literature I
have ever read. He is a shining example of the fact that no matter
what your spiritual background, you can and should elevate your
understanding of the human condition beyond mythology, super-
stition, and magic.
http://www.merton.org/

Joel S. Goldsmith

Emerging from the Christian Science tradition, Joel S. Goldsmith

(1892–1964) was a Christian mystic and healer. In essence, he teaches that God is not Santa Claus and prayer should never be a request for goods and services in exchange for good behavior. He believes that we should refrain from seeking our True Selves in order to fulfill an agenda or pre-conditioned purpose, as this will limit how fully we can realize our true nature. My own self-awareness work took a profound leap once I let go of my expectations of what progress should or could be.
http://www.joelgoldsmith.com/

Eckhart Tolle

I generally try to stay away from the New Age stuff, simply because it smacks of Ego camouflaged as true teaching, but Tolle's bestselling book, *The Power of Now,* is a super-rich resource for learning how to be present—where Ego can't exist—and why that's crucial. The book is filled with very practical techniques for staying in the "now," and is a fountain of ideas about how to become self-aware (though you may want to take some of the "woo-woo" New Age stuff with a grain of salt).
https://www.eckharttolle.com/

PROSPECTING

PROSPECTING AND COLD CALLING are probably the most intimidating words in the sales lexicon. So let's spend a few minutes exploring these important sales responsibilities in order to assuage any fear that may be associated with them.

The entire sales process is often described in terms of prospecting and cold calling—yet these are really just a small part of the much bigger sales process. I am not minimizing the importance of these two skills; they are the foundation of the sales funnel. But I urge you to keep them in proper perspective.

Question: *How do you eat an elephant?*
Answer: *One bite at a time.*

The full selling process can seem like eating an elephant—so daunting that you are tempted to quit before taking your first bite. But when broken down into a series of steps, the process is much more manageable. One of the primary reasons that salespeople fail is that they mistakenly attempt to compress the whole sales process into a thirty-second cold call!

Another reason salespeople fail is the inherent difficulty of introducing oneself to people and gaining their trust in thirty seconds. We will deal with this in more detail as we go along, but for now, please know that it is possible and much easier than you may think.

The first thing you must understand about prospecting is its limited purpose. Prospecting is nothing more than a lead-development process for the purpose of conducting a professional sales call. It is not a process for making a sale.

Understanding this should make prospecting much less intimidating. All you are doing on a cold call is trying to make an appointment to begin your sales call. Keep it simple.

Three Major Components of Prospecting

Prospecting is a vital part of the sales process. It is difficult, but it is good for you. It fills your sales funnel, and you cannot maintain a successful sales career without it. The gratification isn't immediate, so you have to trust that the behavior is worthwhile. You have to believe that the thrill of closing a sale will make all the prospecting and cold calling worth the trouble.

There are three major components of prospecting. Master them completely and your fear of prospecting will diminish greatly.

- Targeting the appropriate customers
- Marketing yourself
- Cold calling

Targeting the Appropriate Customers

It is pretty common for salespeople to have a list of targets. Sometimes this list is called a "Wish List" or "Top Ten List." Those are fine, but in order to excel at prospecting, your list needs to be nuanced, and you need to be very precise in developing it. It needs to have a specific number of prospects and be workable within a specific time frame appropriate for your industry. The phone book does not count as a list. I am sure that EVERYONE would benefit from your product or service, but the phone book is not what we are after here

In his book, *New Sales. Simplified*, Mike Weinberg instructs all salespeople to make a list of targets as a first step for prospecting. He then offers three fantastic ideas for developing this target list.

First, says Weinberg, take a look at your best existing customers and come up with a list of characteristics and traits they share. Then target other businesses that share those same characteristics and traits. Add the best targets to your list.

Another idea Weinberg offers has to do with secondary customer referrals. Getting referrals from customers that you have already sold to is standard, and you should always be doing that, but Weinberg takes the concept further. *Secondary* customers, he points out, can be excellent referral sources. For example, mortgage lenders can target realtors to get them to refer home-buyers; trucking companies might target suppliers of manufacturing goods to urge them to suggest to their customers which trucking company to use. And so on. Sometimes the indirect approach can be much more effective than the direct one.

Weinberg also recommends utilizing resources such as the American Cities Business Journals (http://acbj.com/) and their Annual Book of Lists (http://www.bizjournals.com/bizbooks/) for comprehensive local market data, or Hoover's (http://www.hoovers.com/) for in-depth corporate data. These resources are treasure troves for your research and prospecting efforts.

Marketing Yourself
Allow me to begin this section by stating that marketing *yourself* is very different from marketing *your product or service*. Marketing yourself is not handing out brochures or company flyers.

Marketing yourself is about introducing yourself to people and showing them that you have integrity, that you are selfless and humble, that you care about your community, that you have manners, and that you are a pleasant person. If you market yourself in this way, people will come to you to do business without your ever having to try to sell them anything.

I have always thought of marketing as a way to reduce the need for cold calling. Basically, the more you market yourself, the less you will have to cold call. Not that you can give up cold calling altogether—but you will certainly have to do it less. Wouldn't it be easier to have people calling you than to have to call them?

A lot of marketing people are in the business of selling systems that play on the overwhelming fear we salespeople have of cold calling. These systems vary in effectiveness, but none of them is a substitute for good old-fashioned cold calling. Eventually, you are going to have to put yourself out there and meet someone for the first time, by phone or in person.

One of the big challenges salespeople face is demonstrating that they have credibility. Your efforts in self-marketing should be focused on gaining credibility so that when you attempt to set up a sales call, the prospect already knows you and believes that you are trustworthy and that you have something valuable to offer.

Marketing yourself is prospecting, so keep your self-marketing focused on your potential prospects. In other words, market yourself in areas where your prospects will see you. Since you have already made your targeted list of prospects, it is time to go to work making contact with the businesses and people on that list.

Here are some suggestions for where and how to market yourself so that your targeted list of prospects can see you, learn about you, respect you, trust you, like you, and ultimately invite you into their world.

- Join trade associations
- Join the chamber of commerce

- Join benevolent organizations
- such as the Rotary Club
- Run for city council or other government positions
- Coach Little League
- Volunteer
- Become a board member of a hospital, bank, or other institution
- Produce a video, blog, podcast, website, or book
- Sponsor and lead events
- Write articles for local magazines and newspapers
- Speak at trade shows
- Join websites and online forums or groups
- Establish a solid and helpful social media presence
- Etc.

Invest time in networking and allow people to see and learn about you. The results may be intangible at first, but over time, these self-marketing efforts will help you overcome the biggest problem you face: the fact that people don't know you. Prospects will not buy from someone they do not know.

Because it is so important, I want to re-emphasize that marketing yourself is different from marketing for your company. I urge you to refrain from "selling" while you are engaged in any of the activities listed above. And remember—you must leave your Ego behind when you take on public roles. Your True Self will garner much more favor than your Ego ever will. The point is to be a good person and let others know you are one. Operating in the present moment from your True Self guarantees a positive experience for everyone.

Cold Calling

I have read many books about cold calling. A lot of them try to take the edge off of this arduous prospecting task by giving it another name. Personally, I do not see the point. You can put lipstick on a pig, but it is still a pig. What I am trying to say is that cold calling sucks. There, I said it.

But every job has its downsides and upsides. When I was sixteen, I worked for a guy who sent me into his back dirt lot to stack and organize hundreds of discarded wooden pallets strewn across an area as big as a football field. I spent two weeks hauling, lifting, and stacking the heavy pallets. It was brutal work—dirty, dusty, buggy, spidery, and back-breaking.

But when I was done, I got to work the rest of the summer inside a cool air-conditioned office selling high-end flooring. It was easy, fun, and lucrative. I made a lot of money that summer and learned a valuable lesson. Sometimes you have to do some grunt work to earn the privilege of doing the fun work.

So let's say you have made a targeted list and you have marketed yourself in your offline or online community as a decent, upstanding person. But still you have to make a cold call. What do you do and what do you say?

Keep in mind that your sole purpose on a cold call is to get an appointment for a sales call, either on the phone or in person. You want to engage the prospect just long enough to get an appointment. That said, this is where some of the work you have done on your sales pitches comes in handy.

If you are in the type of sales that requires you to get past some sort of gatekeeper, I have two suggestions. The first is to do enough research to learn the decision-maker's name and position within the company prior to your call or visit. That way you'll know exactly who you are looking for and can craft a question only he or she can answer. This approach gets you past the gatekeeper the majority of the time.

My second suggestion is to read the prospecting chapter in Jeffrey Gitomer's *Little Red Book of Sales Answers*. Gitomer is a fearless New York City-style sales guy who offers an array of creative ways to get around a gatekeeper, including:

- Knowing the name of the decision-maker and asking for him
- Having a good response to the gatekeeper's question, "What is this in reference to?"
- Being friendly, sincere, and truthful
- Asking for help (people are generally inclined to help when asked)
- Being ready with a couple of great questions, such as:
  - *Have you ever considered the top three mistakes people make when purchasing?*
  - *What is the first thing that comes to your mind when you consider the last time you purchased?*
- Send an e-mail announcing your impending visit prior to showing up or calling.

Once you've gotten past the gatekeeper and have the attention of the decision-maker, you simply ask for an appointment to conduct a proper professional sales call—and then you leave or hang up the phone. Keep it tight and simple. You are letting the prospect know that you respect his time and know what you are doing.

When it comes to cold calling, I have saved the best advice for last. I learned my all-time favorite and super successful approach to making a cold call from Stephen Schiffman, who is very well known in the sales-training world and has written over 50 books. He calls this technique "The Ledge."

The Ledge makes it possible to turn just about anything a prospect says into a request for a sales call appointment. Moreover, it keeps you focused on the purpose of the cold call, which is

The power of The Ledge is in its simplicity. Here is how it works. No matter what the prospect says, you simply turn it around and ask for meeting. Here are a few examples.

> **You:** *Good morning Mr. Prospect, my name is Max Seller. I represent ABC Computer Software Company. Companies like yours like us because we have differentiators 1, 2, and 3. May I ask you a question?*
>
> **Prospect:** *Oh, no thanks, we have plenty of software.*
>
> *You: Is that right? Well, lots of companies say that before they get a chance to see ours in action. We should really set up a meeting so I can ask you a few questions and understand your situation better. Does next Monday at 10:00 a.m. sound good?*
>
> **Prospect:** *What is the price?*
>
> *You: Our prices, range from A to B.*
>
> *Prospect: That is far too expensive.*
>
> *You: Well, I am working with a company right now that said the same thing. That's why we should get together.*
>
> **Prospect:** *We only use XYZ Company.*
>
> *You: Sure. I can see that. But, that's why we should set up a meeting. Because many of our other clients said the same thing until they found out how well we complement XYZ Company.*

Prospect: *We just spent our budget for the year on another company like yours.*

You: *That's interesting. Based on what you are telling me, I think we should get together. Other companies have discovered how well we work with other programs like the one you are using now. What does next Tuesday at 3:00 p.m. look like?*

Of all the cold calling strategies I have ever tried, Schiffman's is hands down the easiest and most successful. Again, all you are trying to do is get an appointment for a sales call. Use whatever the prospect says and turn it around to set the appointment.

There are hundreds of cold calling books and specialists out there. Read as many as you can to find an approach that works for you, but (one more time), do yourself a favor and keep in mind that the sole purpose of prospecting and cold calling is to set an appointment for a sales call.

If you hate cold calling, then you'll just have to market yourself even more vigorously, in every way you can think of, so that more people and businesses get to know you. And always start with a targeted list of prospects. This keeps you laser-focused and dialed in so you don't waste time flailing around trying a dozen different approaches to accomplish that simple task: *getting the appointment.*

THE SALES CALL

NOW THAT WE HAVE COVERED THE FUNDAMENTALS and prospecting, it is time to tackle the sales call.

The main function of a salesperson is to sell value to people who need it. Fortunately, almost all people need things and generally seek the greatest value in the things they need. Whether the call is formal or informal, its phases remain the same. Understanding them and moving through them in a disciplined manner makes you a professional and will lead to a successful sales career.

Sadly, there are legions of salespeople and account managers who have no idea how to conduct a professional sales call. It's not that it is so difficult, but most salespeople lack effective training.

This makes it difficult for the rest of us: The hacks are out there every day making a bad name for the true professionals. So, when we show up to execute a proper sales call, the prospect presumes that we are going to waste his time, just as that other clown did last week.

What can we do about it? For one thing, we must train hard and learn to establish ourselves as professionals from the moment the door opens. We must get ahead of that snap judgment. It can be done, but it takes discipline, courage, and lots of practice.

My first sales calls were neighborhood newspaper solicitations when I was nine years old. Each paperboy in the area had a territory, so we knew exactly who was getting the paper and who wasn't.

Every month or so, I would knock on the doors of the non-subscribers and simply ask whoever answered if they wanted the newspaper. Most said no, and off I went to the next house. I wanted to increase the subscriptions in my territory, but I was not doing a very good job of it. I wondered what I was doing wrong.

My dad was a veteran salesman (and easily the best salesperson who ever lived, in my unbiased opinion). So I went to him for advice. He told me that I had to offer something that the customer could appreciate—some kind of personal service.

That made sense, so I worked up a new pitch and headed back out. When a prospect opened the door, I would say, "Good evening, sir [or ma'am]. I am your local paperboy. Beginning tomorrow, I can deliver a dry newspaper to your front doorstep by 6:00 a.m. every morning, if you like. No searching the bushes for your paper. No soggy, rain-soaked papers."

Needless to say, I began to have much more success.

It helped that I was a precocious kid, but all the proper sales-call elements were there. I exhibited an understanding of the customer's point of view, solved a problem, made the service personal, added a little humor, and—BLAMMO—I closed the sale.

Surely you can do as well as my nine-year-old self with just a little bit of study and some disciplined use of the key sales-call elements.

There are five phases to a successful sales call.

- Planning
- Opening
- Probing
- Selling
- Closing

Let's explore each one in turn.

PHASE ONE: PLANNING

GREAT PLANNERS MAKE GREAT SALESPEOPLE.

Whether you are prospecting, presenting, or making multiple sales calls to the same customer, take the time to plan every detail of every call. If you do this, you are sure to impress your prospects and blow away your competition.

Would it surprise you to learn that the majority of all salespeople have no plan, do little or no research, and spend most of the sales call talking about how great they are or how great their company is? They ask very few questions, and—no surprise here—experience very little success.

Critical Point: Be a professional. Plan your sales call.

Research Your Prospect

The Internet is filled with information on your prospect and your prospect's company, so dive in. Discover the issues most important to him and come up with something that might help resolve those issues.

Start by exploring the company's own website, then move on to any personal websites or social media accounts to which you can gain access, including LinkedIn and Facebook. After that, you can widen your search to Google and other search engines.

You are probably well versed in this process, but don't forget to exploit it fully. In fact, your prospect will probably assume that you've done this kind of "Google stalking" … so by all means, do it.

As a side note, this kind of research cuts both ways. Be aware that your prospect may be checking you out in a similar fashion. Tend your own online presence (and that of your company) very carefully. You never know who might be digging around the Internet for the scoop on you, but it is a safe bet that your potential customers will be among them.

An important part of your research should include attempting to discover if a prospect is trying to answer Peter Drucker's Five Most Important Questions Every Business Leader Needs to Answer for Himself. We went over these in the Fundamentals section. As the seller, knowing these evergreen questions gives you an advantage.

If your research reveals that the prospect does not know he should be asking these questions of his own business, you can offer incredible leadership and insight by alluding to them in various ways.

If your research leads you to believe that the prospect is aware of these important questions and is actively trying to answer them, you can still allude to them as a way of showing that you understand the challenges he faces and can offer assistance. This gives you instant credibility.

I thought it might be a good idea to list them again:

- What is your mission?
- Who is your customer?
- What does your customer value?
- What are your results?
- What is your plan?

Keep in mind that your potential clients are extremely busy, furiously attempting to keep their businesses running efficiently and their lives on track. They do not have time to waste. Try to figure out the answers to these questions for yourself prior to your sales call, and then confirm your conclusions during your interaction.

Remember, the questions above are questions that every business leader should have answered long ago about his company. Your purpose in attempting to answer them is a shortcut study method for discovering deep insights into the prospect's operation. This is a great way to build rapport and let the customer know that you are a serious professional, not a glib huckster planning to waste his time.

As you research your prospect, looking for the answers to these questions, the bonus is that you will stumble onto all sorts of random information that may help you connect with him in meaningful ways. Is he from your hometown? Was he in the same fraternity you were? It is almost like cheating to find these things out and then drop them into the conversation.

Well, it *is* a kind of cheating—but the good kind. And in today's environment, it is not a shock when you have some facts at your fingertips on the first "date."

Remember, too, the Five Most Important Questions Every Salesperson Needs to Answer During the Sales Process. We will get into this more during the probing sections later, but it is never too early to learn this information. It is necessary for ultimately closing the sale.

What is the buyer's problem or issue that needs solving?
- What is the buyer's budget?
- What is the buyer's buying process and why?
- Who is making the decisions?
- What is the buyer's timeframe?

Again, do your best to discover this information during your planning research. This is yet another powerful study method, a way to learn your prospect's deepest secrets before you even walk in the door. You will not always figure out the answers beforehand, but when you do, you will be that much further ahead in the sales process.

It is amazing how much information you can gather by starting your research with these questions in mind. Again, you may not be able to answer all of them prior to the sales call, but using them as a basis for your research and planning will pay huge dividends by taking you much deeper much faster.

Determine Your Sales Call Objective and a Backup Objective

If you are prospecting or cold calling, your only objective should be to make an appointment for a later date.

If you are on a sales call that you've previously set up, your objective should be one or all of the following, depending on the complexity of the sale. (Important Note: Always work in this order. Never move on to the next step without completing and then reviewing the one before it.)

- Build Rapport
- Probe for prospect's needs/pains/problems
- Probe for budget (or lack thereof)
- Probe for decision-makers
- Obtain post-probing agreement
- Make your sales presentation or sales pitch
- Close the sale

If you have probed effectively and obtained an agreement from the prospect to make a decision, yes or no ("maybes" are not allowed), then and only then should your objective be to close.

Prepare an Agenda

Always prepare an agenda for the meeting. It provides a roadmap and keeps both you and the buyer on task. It also proves that you are a serious professional who doesn't want to waste your own time or that of your clients.

Your agenda does not have to be complicated. In fact, it should be nothing more than a list of objectives for that meeting. It is important that you share it with the buyer at the beginning of the meeting (or even e-mail it to him ahead of time). If you feel a written agenda is too formal, have an agenda prepared in your mind and state it to the client at the start.

Now that you have done your research, planned your sales call, and created your agenda, you are ready to visit with the prospect.

PHASE TWO: OPENING

THE OPENING OF A SALES CALL SETS THE TONE and builds trust between the buyer and the seller. It also provides guidelines and rules that establish psychological safety, organization, and control of the meeting.

The difference between closing a sale and not closing it is a matter of inches. Every little thing counts. Telling an inappropriate joke, talking too quickly or too slowly, offering a limp handshake—anything at all can derail the sale.

On the plus side, building solid rapport with your prospect right from the start can outweigh a lot of mistakes down the road. Take your time at the beginning (but not too much time!) to set a productive tone and cement your relationship.

Pleasing Personality

There is something critically important I need to mention now that may seem to go without saying. Dale Carnegie wrote about it in his classic book *How to Win Friends and Influence People*—a book that you may want to read or reread as part of this process.

As Carnegie put it, if you do not have one already, you must develop a "pleasing personality." The best and easiest way to do that? It all goes back to the idea of operating from your True Self.

No one likes an egotistic, self-centered jerk who interrupts and talks over people. Pay attention to others and their needs and you won't be that person. And what did I say at the beginning of this book? For your own sake and that of your customers, please, shut that big yapper in the middle of your face. It's no coincidence that you were born with two ears and one mouth. Listen at least twice as much as you talk.

Build Rapport

In your research, you may have discovered that you and your prospect share similar interests, common acquaintances, or backgrounds (schools, cities, organizations, etc.). Use these points of connection as small-talk icebreakers to build rapport and trust.

And keep your eyes open. What do the pictures in his office tell you about where he likes to vacation and how many children he has? What books are on his shelves? What trophies or awards? Feel free to make (diplomatic) comments on any of these things, as a way of revealing your empathy, your personal interest in him and his well-being, and your common ground.

I once Googled a notoriously difficult prospect and discovered that he was very involved in Crossfit Training. I mentioned it during our introductions and he ended up talking to me for an hour about it. It was a fantastic way to build rapport with him.

Here's an old trick from the study of Body Language: Mirror but do not mimic. Notice how your prospect is sitting or speaking and mirror his style. If he is serious, be serious. If he is casual, be casual. But comport yourself naturally, in your own way. (Incidentally, this and many other techniques I discuss here work as well at a party or a bar as they do in a conference room. But that is another book entirely!)

A word of caution: Most professionals are wise to this sort of tactic, so don't tip your hand. Be very natural and friendly and honest, and never bring up anything that you do not know something about. If you see a mounted marlin on the wall but know nothing about fishing, feel free to admire it ... but don't pretend to be a fellow angler. Better yet, leave it alone and find something else that connects you.

Here are some examples of questions from Gerhard Gschwandt-ner's *Sales Questions That Close Every Deal.* These inspire me, so maybe they'll work for you as well, as you strive to build rapport with your prospect.

- I have read that you are a real expert in_____.
  How did you get started?
- What is it the best part of your job?
- Sounds like you have been traveling a fair amount. Do you like traveling?
- I hear you just received a new promotion.
  How do you like your new position?
- I like your name. Tell me its origin.
- I have always wondered about your company name.
  What is the story of that name?
- I read that your company has an interesting beginning. Who was the founder?
- Your team appears so productive and pleasant. How do you keep them motivated?
- Your company is in the news a lot. How do you stay so innovative?
- I just read about your industry award.
  Congratulations. What was the key to getting it?
- I see you graduated from_____. It takes a lot of fortitude to complete a degree like that. What was your major?
- I like the flow of your office space.
  Did you design it?
- Did you see the game last night?
  What did you think?
- Are you still on the Chamber of Commerce board?

You seem to have super powers when it comes to your community involvement. How do you manage it all?

- Look at that clean desk! It is so organized! How do you manage your time so efficiently?
- The word on the street is that you are the most respected manager in the company. How do you do it?
- I brought with me the article about you in the trade newspaper. How do you get such great publicity?
- How do you stay so calm with all the pressure you are under?
- Is that your golfing trophy? What did you shoot to win it?

Propose an Agenda

When the small talk naturally dies down, it is time to take charge of the sales call by stating your agenda. Assure the prospect of the benefits of accepting and following your agenda, then verify that he's on board by asking him if its acceptable, or if he has anything to add. Even if you sent him the agenda prior to the meeting, it's a good idea to recap it quickly in person.

Here's an example of how to present your agenda in a first meeting:

Seller: *Thank you for taking the time to meet with me. In our first meeting, I would like to discover a little more about your operation to see if our service/product matches your needs. Would that be okay?*

Prospect: *Sure.*

Seller: *Great. In preparation for today, I read your mission statement. Can you tell me how you arrived at it? Do you face any challenges in attempting to stay true to this mission?*

Here's a version that might work when you have previously
met with the prospect:

Seller: *In our last meeting, we discussed some of the issues you
are dealing with in your current situation. [Review those issues
in detail before moving on to the budget step.] My experience
with companies like yours leads me to believe that you have a
number of decision-makers and a strict time schedule within
which to make buying decisions. I would like to take the next
thirty minutes to discuss your company's budget for this project.
How does that sound?*

Notice that the presentation of the agenda always ends with
a question. This is a way to secure a buy-in from the prospect.
Remember, in order to stay in control of the sales call, you must
be the questioner—so it's best to include a question at the close
of every statement. Here are some further examples of effective
agenda questions:

- I drafted a brief agenda for today's meeting.
  Would you mind if we reviewed it?
- My purpose for visiting with you today is to ask you
  some questions related to the productivity of your
  computer operation. Is there anyone other than you who
  would be interested in discussing this?
- Thank you for taking the time to discuss your needs for
  improved service. Have there been any changes since we
  last talked?
- My purpose for this visit is to discuss the
  possibility of you working with us again as a
  satisfied customer. Does that sound good?

- The reason for my call is to ask about your needs for greater profitability. Am I right in assuming that this is an area with potential for improvement?
- Before we begin, I am interested in knowing how your situation has changed since our last meeting.
- It is always a pleasure to visit with you. Can we start out by looking over this agenda?
- Before I begin, can we review the progress that we have made thus far?
- Can we quickly review the purpose of our meeting today?
- I know that time is short today. Could you tell me your three most important concerns about your system?
- Could we quickly review the items we discussed on the phone prior to setting up this meeting?
- I was hoping we could discuss your budget process today. Does that sound okay?
- I would really like to achieve a better understanding of your specific needs. Would you be kind enough to share the specifics of your new plan, so I can develop a proposal that makes sense for your operation?
- I drafted an agenda today that includes asking you a few questions that can help me understand your needs. Would you mind if I asked them now?
- So I don't bore you with my presentation, could I ask a few questions?
- Every business has specific needs. May I clear up a few issues with you today?
- My priority is to discover how I can best be of use to you

and how I can help you with your problem. May I ask
you a few questions?

- Your expertise in this field is unquestioned. Do you mind
if I ask you a few questions about_____?

You are doing great. You have presented your agenda and
received buy-in from your prospects. Most important, you have
established control, needs, and pains. Let the probing begin.

PHASE THREE: PROBING

IT'S EXTREMELY IMPORTANT THAT YOU, as the seller, build a clear, complete, mutual understanding of your customer's needs. This will go a long way toward solidifying the power dynamics of this and any future sales calls.

Toward that end, make sure you have some relevant, probing questions organized prior to the sales call. Your main goal during the *probing* phase of the call is to gather information and reveal needs, pains, issues, and problems.

Stay in this probing phase until the prospect becomes emotional about his situation. Asking effective questions establishes positive power dynamics for you, the seller, projects confidence, and sets you up as a leader.

David Sandler, one of my favorite sales trainers and a truly gifted teacher, suggests that salespeople probe in three areas and then establish a post-probing agreement prior to making a sales presentation. He emphasizes that probing must be completed in one area before you move on to the next.

The essential probing steps for any professional salesperson are:
1. Probe for Pain
2. Probe for Budget
3. Probe for Decision-Makers
4. Establish the Post-Probing Agreement

There is an old joke that illustrates why it is necessary to move through the probing steps in order.

A man left his cat with his brother while he went on vacation.
A week later, he came back and called his brother to see when

he could pick the cat up. The brother hesitated, and then said, "I'm so sorry, but while you were away, the cat died."

The man was very upset. "You know, you could have broken the news to me more gently than that!" he said. "When I called, you could have said he was on the roof and wouldn't come down. Then when I called the next day, you could have said that he had fallen off and the vet was working on patching him up. And when I called the third day, you could have said he passed away."

The brother thought about it and apologized.

"So how's Mom?" asked the man.

After a moment of silence, the brother said, "She's on the roof and won't come down."

The point is that it is important how you move from one topic to another in a sales call. If you move directly from the rapport-building phase to talking about money—or worse, making a presentation—you'll lose ground. You might even lose the sale. You've moved much too quickly. Just as on a first date, you have to be cool and not push too hard. Do yourself a favor and be patient. Paint your sales picture one step at a time.

Questioning Techniques

Let me repeat: Be patient as you work your way through the probing steps. Be thorough and detailed. Use the questions you've prepared to control the flow and direction of the meeting. Remember, great questions are a fundamental part of sales.

Understanding the nuances of how, when, and why to use questions will keep you in the driver's seat at every meeting and set you up as a professional worthy of respect, not just a lowly snake-oil salesman. Here are some tips and tricks that will help you move smoothly through the probing process.

Open Questions

Open questions are questions that have to be answered with more than one word. They are meant to "open up" the conversation, to get the prospect talking so that he will feel relaxed and in control of the selling process. These open questions are designed to invite free responses and build trust. Notice how difficult it is to answer them with a simple yes, no, or annoyed grunt.

How did your company get started?

If you could have any business super power, what would it be?

What does success look like a year after installing a new system? How about three years?

What is one thing you would like to come away with today?

Closed Questions

Closed questions are those that can be answered with one word or a short phrase. These tend to focus or "close in" the direction of the conversation.

Closed questions are useful when it is time to confirm your prospect's needs. They are best employed when the prospect is in the flow of expressing his or her ideas, needs, and desires. They are also important as triggers for active listening. Here are some examples:

Are you saying that if we met your essential requirements, you could make a decision today?

Just to clarify, you need more speed and reliability. Is that right?

So, you are saying, sometimes less is more, correct?

Is that the basis of your argument?

Other Types of Questions

Use analyzing, speculating, or compare-and-contrast questions to clarify and catalyze deeper thinking. Your goal here is to dig deep and get the prospect talking. Sometimes it takes these types of questions to get things rolling.

- Here are some examples:
- If you had that capacity, how would things change for you in the next year?
- How does option A compare with option B?
- If we could deliver option A within thirty days, what would that do for your production output?
- What if your overall expenses went down despite a more expensive option up front?

Active Listening

Active listening is a technique used to keep the prospect talking. It confirms your interest and understanding of what the buyer is saying and can be signaled by something as subtle as a well-timed "uh-huh" or as obvious as a complete rephrasing of the customer's words. Try not to use the same confirming phrase more than once.

I know a guy who uses the same two active listening phrases over and over. He either says, "Is that right?" or, "You don't say?" He is genuinely listening and interested, but somewhere along the way he fell into a rut in his speech pattern. It is amusing to listen to in friendly conversation—even rather charming—but it's really not appropriate or effective in a selling situation. Don't be that guy.

You can and must do better.

Here are some examples of active listening phrases:
- "Interesting, say more."
- "No kidding!"
- "Uh-huh."
- "No!"
- "Yes!"
- "Wait, wait, wait … so you're telling me …"
- "Well, I never heard of such a thing."

Probing Techniques

Now that we have the basics of questioning and active listening techniques out of the way, we need to cover probing techniques. During the probing phases of a sales call, you are seeking very specific information.

Before you can deliver your sales pitch, you must discover what your prospect's needs and pains are, how much they are willing to spend, and who makes the decisions. Without this knowledge, your chances of closing the sale are greatly reduced.

Probe for Pain

Go back to your Five Most Important Questions for Any Business. These are real questions that every successful business leader struggles to answer for himself. Your purpose for using these as a study guide is to learn about the prospect. You could ask these questions, but it is probably more appropriate to ask questions related to these questions. Create your own specific questions using these as a starting point.
- What is your mission?
- Who is your customer?

- What does your customer value?
- What are your results?
- What is your plan?

Now, your mama may have told you to stop being so emotional, but when it comes to selling, emotions are the key to a successful outcome. Great salespeople listen for issues, pains, problems, needs, and priorities. Then they dig deeper into them. Do not be afraid to "pick at the scabs" left by previous vendors. Poke the bear. Where is the emotion? Look for eye rolls, scoffs, deep breaths, scowls, etc.

Be patient. Wait until you have struck real emotional distress before discussing the budget, before attempting to find out who the decision-makers are, and before presenting a proposal or sales pitch.

Generally speaking, people make decisions intellectually, but they buy emotionally. The biggest mistake most salespeople make is that they try to sell intellectually. An intellectual conversation with a prospect almost always ends with an intellectual negotiation on price.

You can have the greatest product or service in the world, a product that offers value off the charts, but if you do not take the time to uncover an emotional state within your prospect via great questions, he will attempt to commodify your product or service. In other words, he will focus on price (or availability) alone.

Here is how your sales call will end if you do not strike an emotional chord within your prospect:

Prospect: *Your product lasts a hundred years with no maintenance?*

Seller: *Yes.*

Prospect: *Awesome. Your product will save me a million dollars a year?*

Seller: *You bet.*
Prospect: *Nice. It comes in ten thousand colors?*
Seller: *Yes indeedlydoo.*
Prospect: *Beautiful. How much does it cost?*

At that point, you are done, D-U-N, done. Your amazing product or service is reduced to a commodity no more valuable than toilet paper or fizzy water.

You probably noticed who was asking the questions in that exchange. It was the prospect. When the prospect is asking the questions, the prospect is in control of the meeting. And when the prospect is in control of the meeting, you are going to end up in a discussion about price. Your intention to sell value has flown straight out the window.

Here is how a polished professional salesperson might handle the situation. Notice how he leads the prospect into an emotional state.

Seller: *How are your customers rating your product?*
Prospect: *Not well.*
Seller: *Oh no, really? Any idea why?*
Prospect: *Our computer system is not user-friendly and we lose track of orders.*
Seller: *Uh-oh. That can't be good.*
Prospect: *No, it isn't. If things don't improve, I am going to lose my job. I am just about ready to blow up the whole system!*
Seller: *If you could design the perfect system, what would be your top three requirements?*

Notice the way the prospect's emotion builds until he admits he'd like to "blow up" the entire computer system. Do you think he is concerned about price at this point? No. He needs a solution and he needs it now.

Here's an important tip: An easy way to lead a prospect into an emotional state is to listen intently to his questions and probe for the reason why he has asked those questions in particular. Sooner or later, most prospects will ask a question regarding something that scares them—and that presents you with an opportunity.

Many salespeople miss these opportunities because they are so identified with their Egos that they spend their precious time showing off for the prospect and proving how much they know about the product they are selling.

Bo-ring.

A prospect's question may very well open the door to exactly what you are seeking—if you are listening actively enough to hear it. Tune in. Here's an example of this scenario:

Context: Your prospect was recently burned by a big vendor that abandoned him as soon as he made the initial purchase of some swanky-doo computer software. He vows never to use another big vendor.

During the probing phase of your sales call with him, he asks you how big your company is.

It is a trap. Do not fall for it. Alarm bells should be ringing in your skull any time your prospect asks a question. Leave your Ego behind and refrain from blathering on about how big and awesome your company is. Think about why he may be asking this question. Probe deeper and find out. Then temper your response accordingly. This is your chance to set your company or service apart from the "big bad vendors" of his past experience.

Staying on the right track in a situation like this takes practice because it is so counter-intuitive for the Ego. But your opportunity to dig into your prospect's emotional state is as close as a simple return question. You might say something like:

That is a great question and I would love to talk about my company, but can you tell me why you asked?

If he doesn't want to show his hand just yet, the prospect might say something like:

I'm just curious.

What then?

This is no problem at all. In fact, it presents you with an opportunity to inject some levity into the exchange while going right for the emotional hot spot.

Uh-oh. My radar is going off. Whenever I hear a question like that one, there is usually a good reason for it. Tell me what your real concerns are regarding my company's size. Has something happened in the past that might make you wonder how big we are?

Two very important things are happening here: You are maintaining control of the meeting, and you are reaching into your prospect's emotions. It takes courage, but it is well worth it.

Once the emotional state is triggered, your prospect will tell you exactly how he wants to be sold, right down to the details of his needs, the needs behind his needs, his must-haves, and his would-be-nice-to-haves. He will tell you exactly how to match those needs with the benefits of your product.

You had better be writing this stuff down, because it will become the basis of your presentation. Besides, you may need this information so you can remind your prospect of this pain if he raises new objections during the presentation phase.

Do not move on to the next step until you see emotion from

the prospect. Save the details about your product or service for later. Once you have closed the sale, there will be plenty of time to educate your customer. Your only goal in this phase is to elicit an emotional pain reaction to the current circumstances. You will only be able to play the hero swooping in to save the day if you know what your customer needs to be saved *from*.

A firefighter friend once told me a story about a fire he helped extinguish, and it illustrates my point beautifully. One day, his crew showed up at a house where flames were leaping out of the rafters. He boldly charged into the house and pulled a man to safety. In a weak voice, the man begged him to save his computer. My friend said he would do it if he could and ran back to fight the blaze.

Inside the burning house, my friend saw the guy's computer next to some framed family photos. He could only grab one thing so instead of scooping up the guy's computer, as he was asked to do, he picked up the pictures. He assumed that they must hold more sentimental value to the man than his computer ever could.

Back outside, he proudly handed the pictures over to the man—but he didn't get the grateful reaction he was hoping for. Instead, the man asked the firefighter why he had saved the pictures and not his computer, as he had asked. It turned out the man had just finished his doctoral thesis and the only copy of it was on that computer, along with copies of the pictures he now held in his soot-covered hands.

The point is that when a prospect is in an emotional state (as the rescued man was), he will tell you exactly what he wants and needs. There is no reason to guess, and it can be dangerous to make assumptions. Your priority should be to solve the problem *as stated by the prospect*—not one that you come up with yourself.

- Here are some sample questions to ask when you are probing for pain:
- Your expertise is unquestioned in the company. Based on your veteran status, what do you need to get the job done?
- You are the professional here. What do you need to be productive?
- Can you tell me more about your operator-training failures?
- Obviously you know this business inside and out. If you could get the perfect product, what would it look like?
- If it was ten years ago and you were just starting out, what is the one thing, the one problem, you would avoid at all costs?
- Have your expectations changed since we talked last?
- If you could invent your own machine, what would it be like?
- If you had an unlimited budget, what would be the ideal solution to your biggest problem?
- Would you paint me a picture of your ideal computer?
- Can you tell me the essential functions that you are interested in having?
- When your team met last, what did they agree on in this area?
- Is there anything we are missing? What else would be nice to have?
- What type of lifespan are you expecting?

- Ideally, what is your expectation?
- What would we need to do to make you a customer for life?
- What purpose would that serve?
- What are your current issues with the product (or service) you are using?
- Do your colleagues need to use this at home or at work?
- You said you have a plan. How does your plan solve the issues in your customer service department?
- Do you currently have industrial grade or consumer quality?
- We have a large selection. What kind of applications are you attempting to address?
- Are we talking Cadillac quality, or are you seeking something a bit less robust?
- What is the root cause?
- Have you heard we solve problems like this?
- What happened?
- How did that happen?
- Why did you call us?
- Have long has this been going on? Why now?
- Have you heard of an ideal solution?
- Genie in a bottle. Three wishes. What is your first wish?
- Do you have a criteria set for evaluating this type of product (or service)?
- What kind of service and support do you currently have?
- What do you expect from your service provider?

- What are your current struggles in this area?
- What type of features do you expect?
- You are king for a day.
  What changes need to be made?
- What can you live with? What can you live without?
- You have a magic wand.
  What are you going to do with it?
- How does your current set-up fall short?
- What challenges are you facing now?

Probe for Budget

Having successfully probed for pain, you have unearthed not only your prospect's need for your product, but also the need *behind* the need. Before moving on to the very important phase—probing for budget—always review those needs with the customer. Then it's time to discuss money and timing.

The most important information to gather during this stage is how much money your prospect has available and when he might expect delivery. Always review the needs of the prospect before moving to this probing section. Here's an example of how to move from the recap to the topic of budget:

> *Mr. Prospect, if you don't mind, I would like to review a couple of things before I move on. You have shared with me problem 1, pain 2, and issue 3. In addition, you have stated that if there were some magical product that could solve regulation 4, pain 5, and problem 6, you would eagerly look into it. Do I have that right?*

> *Mr. Prospect, I think I may have the solution to your problems—*

but before we get down to specifics, would you mind telling me what kind of budget you have in mind? Feel free to give me ballpark numbers; you don't have to be specific. I won't hold you to anything.

If the prospect is reluctant to share his budget numbers with you, simply reframe the question. For instance, "Is it less than $10K or more than $10K?"

In this probing step, you are qualifying the customer. The last thing you want to do is launch into a full presentation, only to find out that the prospect has nowhere near the budget to cover the cost of your product or service. Better to know now rather than later.

And here's an important note: Never reduce your price. (For more on this, you might want to read Mark Hunter's *High Value Selling*.) If price comes up, remind the prospect of the emotional distress just revealed and the needs behind the needs. If you were patient during the Pain Probing phase, price should not be an issue here.

Timing can be a significant factor, too. Perhaps your product has a thirty-day production cycle and your prospect needs it today. Perhaps your prospect will not be fully funded for another six months and you are ready to deliver tomorrow. It's better to know now that your timeline is not in sync with the prospect's before you waste any more time attempting to put a square peg in a round hole.

Here are some sample budget questions that you can use to inspire your own.

- What type of budget do you have planned for this?
- Let's pretend that you like what you see
  when I come to demonstrate our product.

Would you be able to purchase our product today?

- How will you fund this project?
- Is financing necessary, or are you ready to pull the trigger?
- Have you considered the financial aspects of this important purchase? What are your expectations in this area?
- In round numbers, how much are you willing to spend?
- Ballpark, what do you expect to pay?
- Historically, who handles the financing part of such a purchase?
- Would you mind sharing the budget you have set aside for this kind of purchase?
- Is there a need for financing for this purchase?
- We have a payment plan. Are you interested?
- Did I mention our financing plan?
- Can we talk about the budget, assuming we have everything you need?
- Rough idea, how much were you thinking this might cost?
- What is your timeline for getting this product in your facility?
- When would you like to get started?
- Is this a down-the-road need or an immediate one?
- Is your company hemorrhaging? Do you need to stop the bleeding right away?
- Our production cycle is substantial; how soon do you need this?

- I can have this on your doorstep in days.
  Do you need it that soon?
- Depending on transportation schedules,
  we could deliver as soon as you want.
  What is your timeframe?
- Approximately when would you need delivery?
- My impression is that you need it within the month. Am
  I right about that?
- I was wondering about your expectations
  for delivery. Soon or not so soon?
- How fast do you need this?
- Are we talking overnight express or snail mail?
- What kind of schedule would we have to meet to satisfy
  your needs?
- By when would you want to have it?
- I am sure you have a timeframe in mind.
  Would you share that information with me?
- Best-case scenario, how soon do you need it?
- Sounds like you may not need this for a while. How
  many months are you from moving forward?
- Sounds like you need this right away. What is the latest
  we could deliver to meet your schedule?

After you have reviewed the problems, pains, and issues and discussed the budget concerns, it is time to begin Decision Probing.

Probe for Decision-Makers

Just as in the last phase, it's important to review what you've discovered before moving on. Go over your prospect's needs and budget one more time. Then prepare to move on to probing for decision-makers. This process makes the next step a natural part of the sale.

Include the prospect in your decision-maker questioning and always ask the question a second or third time to confirm the answer. For example:

Mr. Prospect, we have discussed your needs, problems, and pains. We have also agreed on a budget for this product/service. Besides you, who are the decision-makers when it comes to purchasing services/products like this?

Just you? Oh, okay, that's fine. I only ask because I know I like to discuss these kinds of purchases with my CEO (or Buyer/VP/wife) before I make a purchase. What's that? Oh, of course, your CEO is also a decision-maker. When can we meet with him or her?

This is another way of qualifying your prospect. You never want to shame him by calling him a liar or calling attention to the fact that he has limited power—but you do want to be sure you are connecting with all of the decision-makers, or your "yes" could turn into a "no" after you're gone.

There is nothing worse than proceeding to the end of the sales process only to discover that all the time and energy you put into this prospect was wasted because his decision was not the ultimate one.

It is important to note that you will have to go through the probing-for-pain and probing-for-budget steps again with each decision-maker. These may seem tiresome or redundant, but unless all of the decision-makers are in an emotional state, you will find yourself regressing right back to a discussion on price.

And that is something you do not want.

It does not have to be difficult to start the probing again with another member of the prospect's team. You can always use the original prospect's emotional state and the problems he exposed as a starting point. Be careful, though. One team member's problem may be completely different from another's.

- Here are a few sample questions to jumpstart your decision-maker conversation.
- Who, other than you, is involved in making the decision to buy this product?
- Who besides you has the authority to approve a purchase for this amount?
- I was wondering, is this type of investment decision made by a group of people in your company, or do you have the sole responsibility for approving this important purchase?
- Is your immediate superior involved in making this decision, or are you the sole decision maker?
- Are there other individuals or groups involved in making this decision, besides you?
- In addition to you, who will have a say in buying this product?
- For purchases like this, I usually find there are others who need to be involved. Would you mind telling me who, in addition to you, will have the final authority to write the check for this purchase?
- How far up the chain of command do we need to take this proposal?
- Are you the sole decision maker, or do we need to check with others?

- Is your purchasing office involved, or do they take direction from you on this decision?
- Regarding the decision-making process, how many people will be involved?
- Am I correct in assuming you have sole budget authority?

When you have revealed all the decision-makers and peeled back the layers of pain and problems for each of them, you will be ready to move on to the *post-probing agreement*.

Post-Probing Agreement
Let's review where we are in the sales call. You are sitting with your prospect. If this is a simple sale, perhaps it is your first meeting. If it is a more complex one, you may have already had several meetings. Either way, you have accomplished the following:

- Planned the meeting
- Built rapport
- Probed for pain, budget, and decision-makers

You still need to give your sales pitch or presentation and close the deal. But before you can do that, you need to exact an agreement from your prospect that he will in fact buy from you, provided your product or service matches his needs.

Important note: This is essentially the close, but it doesn't come off as a closing move if you do it before the presentation or pitch. This way you make the buyer feel as if he is *buying* rather than *being sold* once the presentation is over. This is critical sales psychology.

Let me give you an example of why taking this step next is

brilliant, and why successful professional salespeople proceed in this way.

In her book *SNAP Selling,* Jill Konrath tells a great story about a call she received from Southwest Airlines, seeking her services. Now, Konrath is a pro who knows better than to make a presentation or answer too many questions before she gets to the bottom of what her prospect is really after.

But when Southwest Airlines called her she completely forgot to slow down and put first things first. She allowed her lust for the big sale to override her extensive training and experience.

As she tells it, Konrath answered every question she was asked during the phone call, did not ask any questions herself, and even promised to e-mail a proposal two days later. Sure enough, she never heard back from Southwest Airlines.

Konrath says that if she had taken a moment to consider what was happening, she would have told Southwest that she needed to call them back so she could prepare and go through the proper steps of a sales call.

Even seasoned pros slip up sometimes, so don't be too concerned if you do. The point is, no matter how good a salesperson you are, you have to work your way through the steps to make the sale.

If you say too much too soon, the prospect will presume he has the whole story and may very well discount your ability to meet his needs. Remember—he is looking for reasons to eliminate some of his suitors.

If you barrel ahead, having no idea what his needs are, where his pain and problems lie, and who will ultimately make the decision, you are bound to get culled. We've all been there. But with training and discipline, you'll never be there again. You can be sure that Jill Konrath learned her lesson.

If you happen to receive a call from your dream client, try to remain calm and follow your sales process. I remember seeing a television interview with Dick Vitale, the well-known college basketball coach and ESPN analyst. Vitale is famous for his high-energy manner and creative but seemingly random rants.

The interviewer asked Vitale if he knew how manic he sounded sometimes. Vitale answered that sometimes he starts talking and notices an annoying sound a few minutes later—and realizes he is still talking! A joke, perhaps, but there's a glimmer of self-awareness in it.

Sometimes a salesperson begins talking and never shuts up. Whether it is because of nerves or fear or just a lack of training, this cannot end well. If you start to hear that "annoying sound," you must eliminate from your mind the notion that if you keep talking things will get better. They will not.

An untrained salesperson goes about his business backwards. He starts with the presentation and then tries to overcome all the objections, misunderstandings, skepticism, and—worst of all— boredom that ensue. In short, he has given away the best part of his sales call for nothing.

This kind of "backwards" sales call is like reading the last chapter of a novel first. It eliminates any suspense or romance; it certainly eliminates any wooing. Yes, I said it. You have not wooed. You must woo.

You must dangle the carrot just out of reach in order to build interest in your product or service. Picture yourself dangling that carrot and leading the prospect forward as he attempts to reach it and satisfy his hunger. That is wooing. And that is a successful sales call.

The way I see it, you have two choices. Either you chase after your prospect or he chases after you. Wouldn't you prefer that second option? How many prospects are you chasing right now? Probably lots. Are any prospects chasing you? If the answer is no, that can change if you acquire SALES AWARENESS.

As I've demonstrated (and as the Konrath anecdote confirms), you can't possibly know what to pitch or present if you haven't worked your way through the probing sections. But once the prospect has become emotional and spilled his secret pains, needs, and desires, you are most of the way home.

You can gently and easily pick them up and present them back to him during your presentation or sales pitch. You can promise to solve his problems, because now you know what they are.

Get an Agreement

So, how can you secure the all-important agreement that your prospect will buy what you are selling if it meets his needs? It won't surprise you that the first thing you must do is review all the phases you've been through so far. Once you've done that, you need only ask some version of this question:

If I could show you that our product or service solves the majority of your problems, would you make a decision today?

If your prospect says no, do not present or pitch. Press him a little and remind him of his pain and needs, but be prepared to graciously move on to the next prospect. Let me say it again, because this can be difficult: If he is non-committal, do not present. Wishy-washy answers are not acceptable.

No "maybes." "We'll see" does not get it done. This takes

courage, and you have to do it gently, but you have to extricate yourself from the meeting without presenting to a prospect who cannot or will not make a decision that day.

Here are some examples of what a non-committal prospect might say, and how you can respond:

Seller: *Mr. Prospect, we have discussed your fervent need to solve your major problem. We have established that our product/service is well within your budget. And we have determined that you are the sole decision-maker. Now, if I can meet all your needs, will you agree to make a decision—yes or no—today?*

Option 1:
Prospect: *That sounds fair, but you may not like my decision.*
Seller: *Great. That is okay. Yes or no today, no maybes. Let's get started.*

Option 2:
Prospect: *If we like what we see, we will get back to you next week.*
Seller: *Mr. Prospect, forgive me, but I have been around the block a few times, and in my world, that just means no. Could we make a deal that if you do not like what you see, you will simply say no, and if you do like what you see, you will say yes? That way, we both know where we stand and we can get back to the business of being productive. What do you say?*
Prospect: *Well, I am not comfortable making a spur-of-moment decision.*
Seller: *That makes a lot of sense, and I certainly would not want you to feel pressured into making a decision. However,*

if things really are as critical as you say they are, then making a decision today, yes or no, would either allow you to begin fixing your problems or free you up to look for a different option. It sounds to me like the situation is critical, and perhaps the time to act is now. So can we agree to make a decision today?

Prospect: *Okay. I will make a decision today.*

Seller: *Sounds good. Let's get started.*

In this situation, another option might be to offer to come back and present at a later date. The important thing is not to move on to the selling phase until you have an agreement that the prospect will make a decision *that day* if everything looks right.

Finally, if the prospect says no and cannot be moved, be polite and exit gracefully. I have been called back many times simply because the prospect respected my manners. Here is how that might go:

Seller: *Mr. Prospect, can we make an agreement that you will make a decision today?*

Prospect: *No. I am sorry. I just can't do that.*

Seller: *Well, I'm sorry to hear that, but it's fine. I would much rather know that now than wonder if we were really going to move forward. Are you sure you will not reconsider? When I asked you about your computer software problems, I thought you were going to blow a gasket. I think we have a wonderful solution to your software crisis.*

Prospect: *No thanks. I just can't promise to commit to anything right now.*

Seller: *All right, then. Here is my card. I hope you'll call if you change your mind. Have a nice day.*

PHASE FOUR: SELLING

LET'S LOOK AT WHAT YOU'VE ACCOMPLISHED SO FAR:

1. You have gained a complete understanding of your prospect's needs and exposed the emotional layers of his pain, problems, and issues.
2. You have discovered his budget, time frame, and the relevant decision-makers.
3. Finally, you have reached an agreement with him to make a decision that day, if the presentation proves that his needs will be met. Again, this is essentially the closing maneuver couched in a way that allows the buyer to feel more in control of the buying decision.

You've accomplished a lot! All that is left to do is match the benefits of your product or service to your prospect's exposed pains, needs, problems, or issues. Now is the time for that sales pitch you worked so hard on (or in the case of a complex sale, the presentation or proposal that your team has worked so hard on).

The key here is to limit your sales pitch or presentation to the benefits that match your prospect's concerns. Make sure you have discovered every possible need and how you might address it prior to sales presentation, and work it in.

What you don't want to do is get bogged down in the features of your product or service at the expense of its benefits.

Features are the characteristics of the product, such as the pixel count on a TV screen. These are very boring to the prospect—like a lesson might be to a school kid counting the minutes until recess—and should be saved for after the sale is complete. There is no need to instruct a prospect on how to use the burglar alarm or what type of allergen filters are available for a house you are trying to sell for $500K. That can come later.

Benefits are the value to the customer. Once you match the benefits of your product or service to the customer's needs, you are home free. Let's say you are a realtor and your probing session reveals that the husband wants a shop in the garage while the wife wants a large claw-foot bathtub. The house may be on the market for $500K, but your job is to sell a $500K garage to the husband and a $500K bathtub to the wife. No sense going on and on about the solar-powered sprinkler system, no matter how cool you think it is.

When you're presenting, style matters—but not as much as sincerity. Deliver your sales presentation with as much enthusiasm and positive energy as is natural for you, but don't put on an act or you risk coming off like a phony. You do not want to scare the prospect with wild eyes and spit flying from your mouth. Give a professional performance, but refrain from bowing afterward in order to keep the focus on the prospect.

As a concluding statement, review (yet again) your prospect's pain and his budget, give a nod to the decision-makers, and remind them that they agreed to make a decision today.

Then ask:

Mr. Prospect, on a scale of one to ten, where do you think you stand regarding a decision today?

The response you get will tell you whether you need to revisit the prospect's pain once more. If you find that you do, do not be afraid to probe for more pain. Stay calm, come awake, and work the system as you have learned it here.

If the prospect says his number is 5 or under, go back to probing.

You missed something.

If the prospect says his number is 6 or over, ask him what he needs to see to get to 10.

Handling Objections and Resolving Customer Concerns During Your Sales Pitch

If you took your time throughout the probing process, all the objections and customer concerns should have been dealt with prior to your presentation. But there's always the possibility that a customer will express a concern during your pitch.

Here are some helpful hints and techniques for dealing with these:

Misunderstanding

The customer thinks you cannot provide a feature or benefit, so you

- Probe to understand and confirm the need behind the concern
- Acknowledge the need behind concern
- Describe relevant features and benefits that address the concern

Skepticism

The customer doubts the value of a feature or benefit, so you

- Probe to understand the concern
- Acknowledge the concern
- Offer relevant proof of the benefit's value

Drawbacks

The customer is dissatisfied with the presence or absence of a feature or benefit, so you

- Probe to understand the concern
- Acknowledge the concern
- Refocus on the bigger picture or outweigh the concern by reminding him of previously accepted benefits

PHASE FIVE: CLOSING THE SALE

THERE ARE MANY SALES PHILOSOPHIES concerning the close, but my suggestion is to keep it simple and allow the prospect to close himself. David Sandler, one of the most dynamic and successful sales trainers of all time, says that only the prospect can close himself or herself. The close is out of your hands.

At the end of your sales pitch or presentation, you reviewed the prospect's pains and needs. You reviewed the budget. You reviewed the decision-makers. And lastly, you reminded the prospect that he agreed to make a decision, yes or no, today.

I can't stress enough that the closing technique I endorse depends heavily on that post-probing agreement you made, so be very sure you get that agreement before you make your pitch. That is essentially the close before the official close, which comes now.

You will hear over and over in sales training books and courses that it is critical for a salesperson to ask for the sale. Don't worry—I totally agree. What you need to understand is that you already asked for the sale *before* you presented or pitched.

I definitely advocate asking for the sale, but before the sales pitch or presentation rather than after it, so the customer feels like he is buying rather than being sold.

All you have to do to close a sale is ask a version of one simple question:

What would you like me to do next?

That's it. Do not make another sound. Do not move a muscle. Allow the prospect to close the sale for himself.

It sounds counterintuitive, but giving this kind of freedom to your prospect encourages him to close the deal without feeling pushed or run over. As the mighty sales guru Zig Ziglar says, "The prospect loves to buy, but hates to be sold."

Closing in this way makes the prospect feel as if he's in control of his own buying decision, rather than vulnerable to being sold. And the great bonus is that by using this technique, you almost certainly avoid the possibility of buyer's remorse and a cancellation later.

CONCLUSION

AT THIS POINT, WE'VE TAKEN A SUCCESSFUL SALES JOURNEY together, so let's look back at our trip.

The essential job of a salesperson is to sell value in the form of differentiation. The value for the buyer is completely dependent on his needs, pains, problems, or issues. Match the benefits of your product or service to these, and you will close more sales than you ever imagined you could.

Be sure you take the time to develop the fundamentals of professional selling. Great questions allow you to stay in control of the sales meeting. They also engage the prospect in an interesting and relevant manner, and position you as the leader. A solid buyer-centric sales pitch matches the client's needs to the benefits of your product or service.

Below are the logical steps to a winning sales system. If you follow these steps one at a time, you can move your prospect easily and naturally through the sales process and land the sale.

For your convenience (and because review is a powerful tool I use in this book as well as on my sales calls), here are the steps one more time:

- Prospect
- Prepare/Plan
- Open
- Probe for Pain, Budget, and Decision-Makers
- Get a Post-Probe Agreement
- Sell
- Close

All successful salespeople use a sales system. Any system is better than no system, but the SALES AWARENESS system is particularly effective because it incorporates three very powerful fundamental principles: self-awareness, great questions, and the techniques for discovering and solving the buyer's needs, pains, problems, and issues.

Each step of this system is important, but SALES AWARENESS underlies them all. If you truly want to be a successful salesperson, you must increase your level of self-awareness.

You must be present in the moment and identify with your True Self, while leaving your Ego at the door. This will put you on the fast track to success in every area of your life. The closest thing to a "magic bullet" you'll find, in business or in life, is SALES AWARENESS. Without it, all the sales techniques in the world won't get you where you want to go.

Be professional.
Be present.
Be patient.
Be in control.

Be successful.

Bibliography

Sales

Carnegie, Dale (2010-08-24). *How To Win Friends and Influence People*. Simon & Schuster.

Cialdini, PhD, Robert B. (2009-05-28). Influence. New York City: HarperCollins (Collins Business Essentials), 2009. HarperCollins.

Freese, Thomas (2013-11-05). *Secrets of Question-Based Selling: How the Most Powerful Tool in Business Can Double Your Sales Results*. Sourcebooks.

Gitomer, Jeffrey (2011-05-02). *Jeffrey Gitomer's Little Red Book of Sales Answers: 99.5 real world answers that make sense, make sales, and MAKE MONEY* (Jeffrey Gitomer's Little Book Series).

Gitomer, Jeffrey (2011-05-02). *Jeffrey Gitomer's Sales Bible: The Ultimate Sales Resource: Including The 10.5 Commandments of Sales*.

Grabher, Alfons (2013-05-29). *The 3 most powerful presentation techniques of Seth Godin*.

Gerhard Gschwandtner (2006-10-11) *Sales Questions That Close Every Deal: 1000 Field-Tested Questions to Increase Your Profits* (SellingPower Library).

Hill, Napoleon (2011-08-10). *Think and Grow Rich* (Gildan Media Corporation).

Hunter, Mark (2012-02-14). *High-Profit Selling: Win the Sale Without Compromising on Price.* AMACOM.

Kennedy, Dan S. (2008-11-17). *The Ultimate Sales Letter.* Adams Media.

Konrath, Jill (2010-05-27). *SNAP Selling: Speed Up Sales and Win More Business with Today's Frazzled Customers.* Penguin Publishing Group.

Maxwell, John C. (2014-10-07). *Good Leaders Ask Great Questions: Your Foundation for Successful Leadership.* Center Street.

Miller, Robert B.; Heiman, Stephen E.; Tuleja, Tad (2008-10-25). *The New Strategic Selling: The Unique Sales System Proven Successful by the World's Best Companies.* Hachette Book Group.

Pink, Daniel H. (2012-12-31). *To Sell Is Human: The Surprising Truth About Moving Others.* Penguin Publishing Group.

Sandler, David; Mattson, David (2015-03-23). *You Can't Teach a Kid to Ride a Bike at a Seminar*, 2nd Edition: *Sandler Training's 7-Step System for Successful Selling.* McGraw-Hill Education.

Schiffman, Stephan (2007-12-01). *Stephan Schiffman's Sales*

Essentials: All You Need to Know to Be a Successful Salesperson-From Cold Calling and Prospecting with E-Mail to Increasing the Buy and Closing. F+W Media, Inc..

Tracy, Brian (2006-07-16). *The Psychology of Selling: Increase Your Sales Faster and Easier Than You Ever Thought Possible*. Thomas Nelson.

Weinberg, Mike (2012-09-04). *New Sales. Simplified: The Essential Handbook for Prospecting and New Business Development*. AMACOM.

Witty, Adam; Kennedy, Dan (2013-10-23). *Book The Business: How To Make BIG MONEY With Your Book Without Even Selling A Single Copy*. Advantage Media Group.

Ziglar, Zig (2007-05-13). *Ziglar on Selling: The Ultimate Handbook for the Complete Sales Professional*. Thomas Nelson.

Self-Awareness
Allen, James (2014-11-01). *As a Man Thinketh*. CreateSpace Independent Publishing Platform.

Carnegie, Dale (2010-08-24). *How To Win Friends and Influence People*. Simon & Schuster.

Dispenza, Joe (2008-10-22). *Evolve Your Brain: The Science of Changing Your Mind*. Health Communications.

Dyer, Wayne (2011-01-01) *Excuses Be Gone! How to Change Lifelong, Self-Defeating Thinking Habits.* Hay House.

Guy, Finley. (2007-10-08) *The Secret of Letting Go.* Llewellyn Publications

Goldsmith, Joel S. (2013-10-02) *The Infinite Way.* CreateSpace Independent Publishing Platform

Hill, Napoleon (2011-08-10). *Think and Grow Rich* (Gildan Media Corporation).

Hawkins, David R. *Power vs. Force.* Veritas Publishing.

Hawkins, David R. (2013-08-01). *Letting Go: The Pathway of Surrender.* Veritas Publishing.

Howard, Vernon (2012-05-31). *The Magic of Your Personal Mind Power.* Melrose Publishing Co..

Krishnamurti, J Jiddu (2007-12-23). *The Collected Works of J. Krishnamurti, Volume 1: The Art of Listening.* Delvensoft.

Krishnamurti, U.G. (2007-09-10). *Mind is a Myth.* Sentient Publications.

Merton, Thomas (1999-10-04). *The Seven Story Mountain.* Mariner Books.

Nightingale, Earl (2007-10-15) *The Essence of Success*. The Richest Man in Babylon.

Plato (2007-12-28). *Classic Philosophy: Complete Dialogues of Plato*. B&R Samizdat Express. Kindle Edition.

Plotinus (2009-12-03). *THE SIX ENNEADS*. Classics-Unbound. Kindle Edition.

Thoreau, Henry David; Ralph Waldo Emerson (2008-01-01). *The Complete Works of Ralph Waldo Emerson & Henry David Thoreau*. C&C Web Press. Kindle Edition.

Tolle, Eckhart (2010-10-06). *The Power of Now: A Guide to Spiritual Enlightenment*. New World Library.

Watts, Alan W (2000-10-05) *What Is Zen?* New World Library.

Wilber, Ken (2001-02-06) *A Brief History of Everything*, 2nd ed. Shambhala.